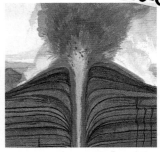

How a Volcano Is Formed

Written by Sandra Iversen
Illustrated by Falcon Halo

If you could travel down into the earth, you would get hotter and hotter. Twenty miles inside the earth, rocks get so hot that they melt.

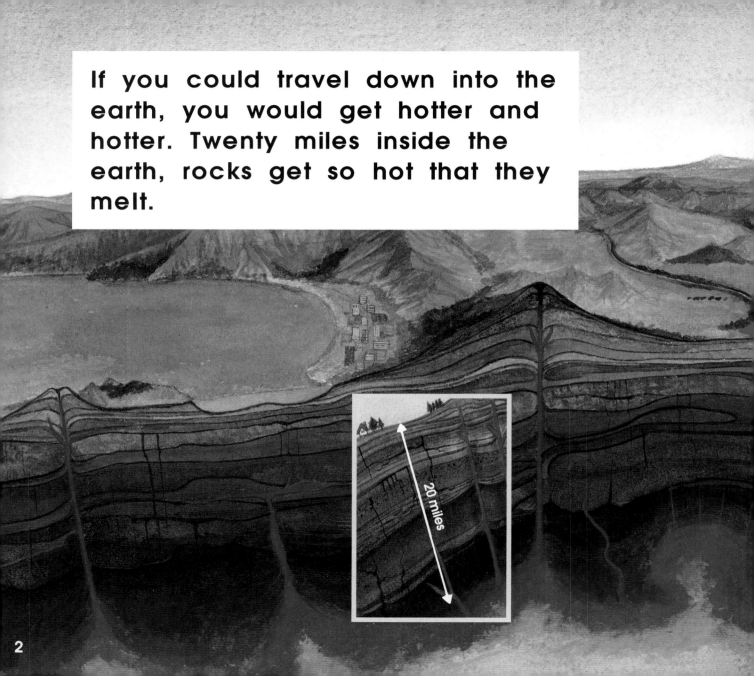

20 miles

When the rocks melt, they expand and need more space.

Sometimes there are cracks inside the earths crust. The melted rock, called magma, spreads into the cracks.

4

If there is too much magma in the cracks, pressure builds up. The magma bursts out of the earth, creating a volcano.

Sometimes volcanoes erupt in the sea and form new islands. Sometimes volcanoes erupt on the land and destroy towns.

Some volcanoes stop erupting. These are called *extinct* volcanoes. Some volcanoes do not erupt for many years. These are called *dormant* volcanoes. Some volcanoes keep erupting. These are called *active* volcanoes.

Today, more than 500 volcanoes around the world are active.